DIARY
of a
RAPE VICTIM
Breaking the Silence to Break Free

By

PHILLIS VAN GODWIN

A division of Squire Publishers, Inc.
4500 College Blvd.
Leawood, KS 66211
1/888/888-7696

Book illustrated by
Lester D. Godwin

Copyright 2000
Printed in the United States

ISBN: 1-58597-053-0

A division of Squire Publishers, Inc.
4500 College Blvd.
Leawood, KS 66211
1/888/888-7696

Acknowledgment

I would like to acknowledge and thank Susan, my therapist. Without Susan there would have been no encouragement to write this book.

I would like to thank my husband for his support through our years of love and hardship together.

To my two sons who supported this effort without embarrassment.

———————

The walls that I have managed to hold together for almost 40 years have crumbled. I stand here in bare shame. I can no longer keep them up.

I didn't write this book to hurt anyone. The intent is to heal and not to hurt.

Phillis Van Godwin

"To thine own self be true."

— *Shakespeare*

• *June 1989 — Remembering …*

It was 1961.

I was running, breathing hard, making quick turns — trying to double back and get back to the car. I wasn't screaming; I tried not to make any noise, hoping he couldn't find me in the darkness. But I could hear him gaining on me, the man who was trying to rape me. As he caught me, he jerked me to the ground. He tore my insides — I screamed, pushed, kicked — fear was gripping every part of my body — finally it was over. I felt violated, soiled and dirty.

* * * * * * * * * *

I'm telling my story because I don't want to be guilty any more. I'm innocent, Daddy. I was afraid he would kill me. I screamed and fought him. I ran, cried, begged and pleaded, but he wouldn't stop. I couldn't make him, Daddy.

I called the police, Daddy. They took me to the hospital. I was torn and bleeding. I went through a trial and told everyone in the community every gory detail. His lawyer tried to make me the guilty one, but the jury found me innocent and sent him to prison.

I'm 46 years old now, Daddy, but I'm still serving time.

• February 21, 1992

It's ironic that I look at my father as a prison warden. But the way I told my story ... he still has the keys.

Since last Friday ... I've allowed myself a lot of tears over this. I've started therapy, and my therapist told me it was all right to have angry feelings. I didn't even have to let anyone know I was feeling anger. So I was able to go take the June 1989 letter out of its hiding place, my old recipe box. I've kept it there almost three years ...

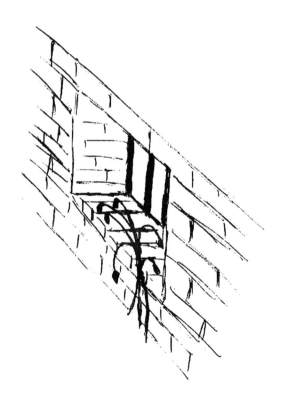

• *February 23, 1992*

I read my rape letter to my therapist. I had never shown it to anyone ... it caused me such pain and embarrassment. I call it "my letter of shame." I still cry every time I read it. I cry for the pain I've carried for 30 years ... the pain of the rape. I cry for the person I would have been, but was unable to be. I cry because I've spent 30 years trying to be someone else.

I've tried so hard to be a person everyone liked. I gave everything 100% of me, but it was never enough. I cry because I used all my strength and all my life trying to make up for the rape. I cry because no one cared to look for the real "me."

Was it the "real me" who was always buying things for people so they would be my friend?

My therapist said, "Quit buying gifts and see how many real friends you have." It is so hard because I may not have any friends.

I remember getting married and being afraid to go for a walk with my husband. I couldn't trust anyone to help me.

Every place I went I looked everywhere for danger. Where could I run if someone attacked me?

We had two sons. They are fine young men, but when I was out alone with them, even when they were in their teens, I was afraid to trust them for my protection.

They never knew. Silence is the word.

> *"I can hear her moaning when she's afraid. She knows not to trust anyone, not even my sons."*

I walk and try to act natural, always talking too much. But I have to talk to cover up the sound of her moaning. When I'm in a group, she can't stand silence. I can hear her pounding on the wall wanting to be heard.

• *February 26, 1992*

I don't understand why the only person interested in what I have to say is a stranger I have to pay.

I understand if it's pink and not blue, that just makes it me and not you. Do people just think I have nothing to share? Do they not have time to spare?

5

I must tell something so painful to me …
I must tell to set me free.
I must tell to break your power over me.

The therapist told me I would have to tell people about "the rape" so they wouldn't be able to use it as a threat over me to tell others.

There is such a feeling of shame in telling people I was raped. They don't know how to react to you. They get nervous.

I never wanted to tell anyone! It hurts too much! It was a secret that was hidden with her. If I didn't talk about it, she didn't have to feel shame. I tried to forget it so she wouldn't be afraid. I didn't want her to be afraid. I didn't want her to be locked away and lonely with no one there with her. But it was the only way I could keep her safe. If I was very careful, she could rest. I just didn't want her to be hurt any more.

Where does tomorrow go? How can I get there? Who will care if I am there? Can I get there going north? Will anyone know if I am there? Will it be different from today? Will getting there make any difference? Will anyone see me there?

• *March 8, 1992*

I can't fix it, and I can't make it right. I'm trying to come out from behind my wall of protection.

Why am I trying to find me? My real person must be so horrible that no one wants her out. What's the use in bringing her out? Why bother? Why try? Why am I putting myself through this? It hurts and it's so painful. No one cares about the real person; they all just want to blame her.

All the blame is keeping her hidden. She cries out in pain and anger, but no one is ever there. So settle her in and get her comfortable, because she may be there forever.

Pull down the blinds and hook all the latches. Do it up right so it will look natural. Then no one will know she's back there.

Tell her she's safe there and it's so much nicer back there. There will be no pain, no yelling. No one will know she's been bad.

But sometimes I cry for her 'cause, you see, I know her. I found her to be so kind. She suffered so much pain, I put her there so she won't hurt any more.

If anyone ever looks for her, I'll tell her. But the shell of the person that I reveal can take all this 'cause she doesn't let her pain show. She doesn't tell her secrets. She's always smiling and trying to make everything right.

Don't wake her, don't shake her, it's all right. It's sometimes lonely back there, but she can hide.

I tried to use the word "nice" to describe her, but I had to cross it out, 'cause no one thinks that. But I thought it and believed it. Of course, that doesn't make it right. But she quit trying and trying to make it all right.

Now she's quiet; she's silent, 'cause she gave up expecting and believing that things would be right.

- *March 10, 1992*

  Yesterday I was so sure I had failed, and in my grief I almost quit trying.

  Today I'm working so hard to erase that guilt deep down inside, so I can quit trying.

  Tomorrow will bring comfort to me, and I'll be able to feel pride in myself and be set free.

- *March 12, 1992*

She sits up there today all alone and tucked away. No one can touch her there for, you see, she's locked away.

I put her there one day so I could put on a mask for all the world to see.

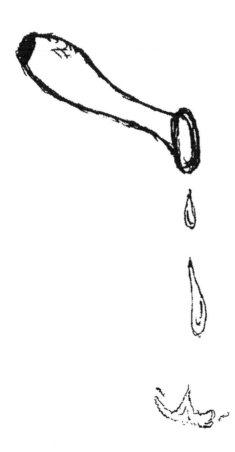

- *March 13, 1992*

I pick up a pen and write these words about pain and life and what they do to me. Sometimes I'm able to share them, but sometimes I'm not. Can I stand to open that door and reveal all that pain?

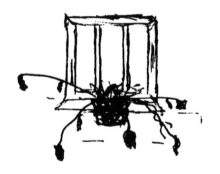

• *March 17, 1992*

If I had known that night I was raped ... that I would be a rape victim forever, and that I would be blamed for going out and getting myself raped ... for the next 30 years, I would never have told anyone ...

I would have suffered in silence, alone. But instead I trusted and reported it, doing all the right things the law says to do.

I opened up my pain and told the whole community in court. But it only brought me punishment, shame and disgrace. He served time in prison. I've served my own time in prison. What did he serve, how many years? I've served 31 years so far ... and I'm still serving.

Today I'm trying to break out of that prison ... but to do that means exposing myself to everyone yet again.

I'm telling myself I should never have told anyone, because telling brought the cost so high to me, so in not telling I would have only suffered the silence. I would have saved myself shame, punishment and disgrace and having to tell it again.

Will it ever end? Will I ever be free of it? How much more do I have to pay? Just how much do you want me to pay? What is the cost to me, to be free of my guilt?

How much must I pay and can I ever be set free? How long must I pay, and which way can I go? Why must I go it alone, because of the trust I gave to you. Is there a right way and a wrong? Did I somewhere fail in finding these?

- *March 18, 1992*

My future seemed so full of sunshine.
My tomorrows were filled with such dreams,
till one day I found … I could only know pain.

I tried to believe in such happiness
that life was much more than a game.
I wanted to just try believing and
trusting that happiness can be without blame.

But dreams are not like sunshine
because most days they don't come true.
There's no pot at the end of the rainbow,
and happiness just is something beyond the blue.

Today was therapy again ...

I sit here and write about families. I just don't understand them. From baby to adult, you're so hooked to them. You grow up thinking you can't live without them. But one day you find you have to separate yourself from them, as you can no longer survive attached to them as you are.

They carry so much pain with them, and to be a part of them — you too have to carry all this pain. They try to play games with your emotions and place guilt if you don't play it their way.

What happens if I don't want to play, if their games seem foolish to me? What happens if I don't play it their way, if it no longer seems right to me?

Am I allowed to quit for awhile, to step back and take a fresh look? NO! They quit associating with me. There's no longer any time for me, so the game continues whether I'm there or not.

They all have to change places when I'm no longer there. The game goes on and the rules continue.

• *March 20, 1992*

I cry for her and weep for her
cause she's out of sight. She has no
power, no control to make everything
right.

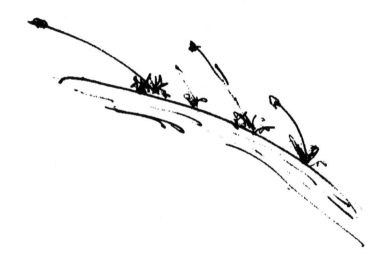

- *March 22, 1992*

Where does tomorrow go? How can I get there? Who will care if I am there? Can I get there going north? Will anyone know if I am there? Will it be different from today? Will getting there make any difference? Will anyone see me there?

I've always believed in summer. I've always thought there would be warmth there. I've always believed the people there were smiling and happy. But when I got there ... I found only pain. People were not happy and could not be pleased. I ached to touch them and make everything right, but when I reached out, they moved away. In my shame I moved within and could not be touched. So ... I never really found warmth there ... and I turned north trying to find winter ... to see if it was different there ... but when I moved away ... they moved on, too.

- *March 23, 1992*

Where do flowers go ... when the bloom dies and they fade away? If I looked under the leaves, would I find them there? Does the ground reach up and pull them there, to keep them covered during the rain and snow? Do they bloom again when the sunshine glows? Or do they die forever under the sleet and snow?

She can't stand to see the flowers cut. She knows they'll just dry up and fade away. She turns her head and cries when they're being cut. In her world the growing flowers are all she's got.

Where will I be when they learn to care?
Where will I go when they don't care?
When will it all end? Who am I and do I care?
Where have I been when it was damp and cold?
If they learn to love, will it be enough?

• *March 24, 1992*

I've always looked for the best in each one, and sometimes I've hunted and found none. But I'll keep on looking to see if someone cares enough to lighten or brighten my way.

One day I learned mistrust when no one would come. I carried it with me just like it was a gun. I didn't feel safe without it; it was my loaded gun. It couldn't be laid down or left alone since no one would come.

Yesterday I had all my dreams. Today brought all my failures. Tomorrow all my hope will come. But where do my tomorrows and yesterdays meet? Since today has brought such sorrow?

Giving my best is never enough,
Singing their praises and all that good stuff.
Buying them presents and going to lunch
just causes me sufferings and all that bad stuff.

My way and their way is never the same;
This way and that way to them is the same,
but somehow ... some day tomorrow will come,
And I'll find out that day from where I've just come.

To one believing is so much fun,
finding hope somewhere is a rule of thumb,
But grey skies and rain clouds ... which tomorrow holds
bring daffodils and rainbows to everyone.

Things I do to survive

1. Keep quiet (always keep quiet)
2. Cry
3. Take sleeping pills
4. Beg and plead on my knees
5. Pray
6. Try to figure out in my mind where I've messed up … so I won't do it again.
7. Put my feelings and emotions behind a wall so **no one** can reach them.
8. Keep telling myself I don't need anyone.
9. (Nearly) always saying "Yes" to people.
10. By telling myself I'm mentally slow is the reason I don't measure up, and that's why people don't really love me.
11. By trusting no one.
12. Trying to act like everyone else.
13. Not telling my problems to people.
14. Believing dreams really come true.
15. Trying to buy friends
16. Not telling "secrets"
17. Not watching anything at the show or on T.V. but "happy endings"
18. Not letting pain show
19. Trying to make everything come out right.
20. Trying to ignore when others hurt me

21. *Keep telling myself it's not important.*
22. *Do anything so people are not angry with me (or whatever it takes)*
23. *Eating last when I'm with a group*
24. *Giving everything I've got (which is never enough)*
25. *Wiping tables at church functions*
26. *Thanking anyone who does something for me.*
27. *By loving animals in place of people.*

- *March 27, 1992*

   By not letting others into her life she could avoid the unbearable pain inside her.

   She can't let down her walls. She's not allowed to feel love because it would just bring her pain. I put her safely away so you can't touch her.

• *March 28, 1992*

I saw my therapist today. She said my smothering attacks that I've had for the last 25 years may be from the rape. They most always occur about one hour to one and a half hours after I go to sleep. It may be a recurring dream that sends my body into a fear panic, which in turn forces my body to push everything I've eaten all day out by either mouth or bowel. I have to get outside where there are no restraints. If there were no doors, I'd go through the wall. I can't breathe until I'm outside.

I can't deal with it! She thinks I'm already trying to deal with it, but says I don't have to remember anything I don't want to. The attacks I've had while I'm awake could be "flashbacks." She said I wouldn't necessarily remember them. The attacks cause me terror, and it's my body's way of fighting them. I'm to keep a journal morning and night, writing my dreams down just as soon as I wake up. I'm also to write my activities of the day down, plus anything different I eat or do each day.

When I have these attacks, I feel I'm not getting any air, so my body goes into overdrive. I'll lie in shorty pajamas in the snow with a 20-below wind chill just so I can get air. My throat swells, and I can't swallow, causing me to nearly pass out — might be connected with this also.

The therapist said, "A shadow of something you don't remember could be worse than the incident once it is brought out into the light.

I started having these attacks right after we moved

23

into Roe Village Apartments. My husband remembered that it was after I found out the "rapist" was out of prison.

My mom simply told me one day on the phone, "We think he's out of prison." I couldn't think who she meant. I don't believe she said anything else. I hung up the phone, and it came to me: **Oh, no!** He'll come after me.

There was no one to talk to. My husband never wanted to talk about it. But I needed someone to listen and someone to share my fears with. I shook every time I thought about him being out of prison.

I will not allow myself to remember!
I will not allow myself to remember!
I will not allow myself to remember!

The attacks cause me terror! They started when he got out of prison! For 25 years I never put the pieces together!

I buried **you, RAPE!** I thought I had you hidden back there so far you could never come out! I nailed the door shut! I never told anyone! I hid you because I didn't want people to think less of me. But you came out in my sleep. I fought you with everything I had. I fought the rapist and lost. I fought the knowledge of you and lost.

I buried you, and you kept coming through. I fixed myself up, I showed a happy face. "Look at her, she's all fixed up and so happy." But underneath you were **screaming** to come out. **I fought you** and believed I had won. Now 31 years later I'm finding out I've been losing all these years!

• *March 31, 1992*

My mom says to me, "He's been set free!" I listen to her and think just what it means to me. I'll wake up at night throwing up and shaking. I'll experience smothering attacks and think I'm dying.

Doctors will run thousands of dollars of tests to find the cause and come up empty-handed.

No one asks what's in my mind. And me ... I think I'm doing fine.

My younger 20-year-old brother was killed in a plane crash.

We flew back to Kansas City from Washington state where we were living. I had babysat him. He was next to me in age. He meant so much to me. A day or two before the funeral my mother said to me, "We've gotten a strange telephone call for you. We believe it's 'him.' "

No one said another word about it. In my grief I tried to think what she meant.

***Oh, no!** Oh, **please,** dear God, he's found me through the obituary they sent to Arkansas. He's been hunting me! He now knows my married name and that I live in Everett, Washington.*

My mind ceased to function. I was in a fog. Grief, fog. Grief, fog. Fog, grief. I didn't know any more what was what. I didn't care. I didn't think I couldn't think.

I waited for him to show up. Where? When?

Cemetery, funeral, my parents' home, where? Will he wait until I get back to Washington?

Sometimes I could hear her screaming behind the safe wall. I couldn't help her! I just let her scream!

If the fog started to lift, she screamed more! There wasn't anyone back there for her to talk to.

When I saw my brother's broken body in the casket, I started screaming with her.

The fog returned. The funeral came and went. The time came, and we put him in the ground. I walked away and left him there. But **"he"** hadn't showed up yet. I was so tired of waiting.

Sometimes now there was nothing from behind the safe wall. I knew she was no longer safe, but I had no place else to put her.

Sometimes when she was quiet, I reinforced the walls to try and make it safer. I built the wall higher and thicker. I would hammer until she would start screaming. I would let her scream day and night; minutes, hours, days, however long it took. When she stopped, I would hammer again.

Finally I kept hammering while she screamed. The louder she screamed, the harder I hammered.

He's dead now ... my mom told me so. Again I listen to her and think what it means to me.

Will this mean no more sickness for me? Does this mean my mind can run free and my dreams can be happy? Does this erase all that's happened to me? But my mind can't comprehend that it is free.

The terror is still coming and attacking me!

- *April 9, 1992*

> *Please don't make me tell it!*
> *Please, the pain, I can't bear it!*
> *Don't tell it! Don't tell it!*
> *She's frantic, she's frantic,*
> *The pain, I can feel it.*

*You sat in the courthouse and heard the horror.
We never talked about it. I was afraid to sleep alone
at night. I was 17 years old. I believed it was all my
fault. Daddy, in your anger one day in 1982 you told
me you were going to tell my grandchildren what I
went out and got done to myself. My mother stood
behind you and didn't think there was anything
wrong with what you said. I was standing in the
doorway of my husband's and my home. I started
screaming!*

*The threat to any grandchildren I might have was
the most painful thing you could have done to me. Are
your feelings about me so bad that you would run me
down to innocent little children?*

*I felt something was so terribly wrong with me. I
tried so hard for your approval. No matter how
wronged I felt, I kept going back. Home and family
are supposed to be safe. You're supposed to find comfort there, but continually going back was destroying
me. I was losing respect for myself.*

*My pain is still there, and the rape is still there. I
can't go on denying them and pretending everything's
okay.*

*Do things that are important to me matter at all
to you? What did you expect me to do, just go on as if
nothing happened? I tried so hard to. When I men-
tioned it to Mom, she said I was making too big a*

deal about it. I came to my end. I could no longer go on.

My mom had told me I make too much of the rape. She told me the rape really hurt her. Excuse me! Really hurt her? How did it really hurt her? Was she really hurting when Daddy told me he was going to tell my grandchildren what I did? She was standing right behind him and didn't say a word.

What were her feelings when she told me he was out of prison? What was she feeling when she told me he was trying to find me?

• *April 14, 1992*

Do you know what it's like to be raped? Do you know what it's like to believe someone is going to kill you? Do you know what it's like to have someone blame you and put you down because of the above? Do you know what it's like to have panic attacks because of the fear you live in for 30 years? Do you know what it's like to be afraid to trust anyone? I know what it's like, and I have no words to describe it to you.

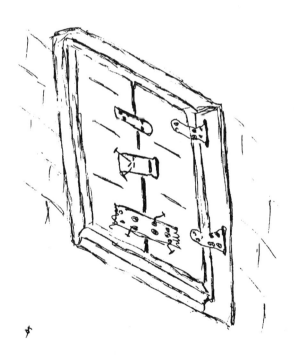

• *April 15, 1992*

I can't acknowledge that the person behind the "safe wall" and me are the same person. I'm trying to trust people. She can trust NO ONE. I try to be happy. She lives in fear and lets no one touch her. I try to love and show love. She doesn't allow herself to do any of these. I walk in the park and try to be cautious. She screams and hides behind the wall.

When I feel I can't go on, there is only silence from her. Sometimes I go to bed and stay for days. That's the only rest she gets. She doesn't like or eat food, but after two or three days I have to get out of bed to drink water and eat something. She wants me to go to bed and not get up.

Look at me *and tell me what you see,*
    a rape victim that will never be set free.
Teach me *so that I will feel shame and*
Threaten me *that you'll tell my grandchildren*
    what you think I've done.

Look at me *and think I'm free,*
    but you can't see what's inside of me,
    Just how my life has been so affected;
    no close friends 'cause they couldn't be trusted.
    Don't touch me, 'cause I'm afraid of touching.
Look at me *and see only the surface*
    'cause underneath there's so much suffering;
    I'll smile and act carefree,
    but that's all you'll see of me.

- *April 15, 1992*

Nights are extremely hard for us. We are both afraid. I can hear her crying softly as evening comes on. It's hard to sleep and listen at the same time. I toss and turn and she cries. We're both listening for any sound. Sometimes I will hear something and my heart will start pounding. I can hear her screaming. The only real rest is sleeping pills. They stop my thinking and her screaming.

• *April 16, 1992*

I had never told my oldest son I had been raped. I knew I had to tell him before someone else did. He was serving in the military. I waited for his release from the Army so I could tell him. And I wasn't sure just how much my younger son knew.

The day finally arrived. My oldest son was out of the military and back home, and my younger son was still living at home. I couldn't put it off any longer. The therapist had told me I had to tell to take the power away from other people.

Do you know how hard it is to tell grown men their mother was raped when she was 17 years old? I was emotionally strung out, almost to the point of being sick. My sons were 28 and 24 years old. The shame was there. I was so afraid they would be ashamed of me. I didn't want to tell them. How un-fair it is to have to tell your children.

- *April 17, 1992*

The therapist told me I had a right to say "No" to things people would ask me. I had to learn to trust again. In a healthy environment people can express their feelings openly. She said "SHAME" keeps situations locked in, and do not disclose to people about yourself because you feel you have to.

I listen to her. I go home and work on it. It's not easy to change things in your life. The "SHAME" part is so hard for me.

I've found that so many people come through your life. It's so hard to trust people. If they find out you've been raped, they have so many questions.

I've found rape changes forever or until the mind is dead.

My therapist said I could bring someone to orientation with me. It would just be for two weeks. She said they would be able to give me support as they would know what I was going through. I don't have anyone to take. No one ever stands up for me. No one wants to hear about the rape for more than a moment or two, so who do I know that would be willing to go sit and listen for three hours (one and a half hours each night)? **Hello out there! Is anyone there** *who would come? Silence ... so I'll ask no one because there's no one to come.*

If your actions are different from your words, take a good look. **I'm not there any more. You may see** *my body sitting there on the sofa, but look inside 'cause I'm gone.* **You can't find me!** *The only way I can be found is through love and caring. If you feel none of these for me, you'll never find me!*

I'm done gone! Do you hear? I'm not there any more. *I tried and tried. I wanted to love you and be one of you. Maybe I didn't know how or maybe I just failed again. But either way it's over for me.*

The therapist says the place I'm in is very difficult because I'm bucking the system.

This week at my session I rambled on and on to my therapist. It was as if I had to talk the whole hour even if there was nothing to say. I knew I was rambling on and even told her, but I couldn't stop.

Go tell the world that you've been raped, but when they hear, they won't think you great. If you tell them, they'll try to place blame, so what do I care what they think.

- *April 22, 1992*

Woke up in the early morning hours. I was tossing and turning. I could hear her crying. She was lonely. There was no one back there but her. What could I say to her? What could I tell her?

You're there for your own good? I don't want you to be hurt any more. I'm trying to keep you safe. Don't you know I'm trying to protect you?

Did I dare tell her she would be back there the rest of my life? Did I dare tell her I was putting bars on all my windows and doors? We were both going to live in prison.

Did she know I heard her crying the last two times my husband and I went for walks in the park? I knew there were men there. I didn't trust them either. As I walked and talked with my husband, I kept looking back to see if one of them was following us. I didn't want her to know I was afraid, too. I can't tell her if someone tries to rape me again, he'll have to kill me.

What would that do to her? She lives in isolation now. She's never, never getting out. I can't stand it when she screams and cries.

Sometimes I think I'm going crazy

just surviving myself. What about her? She has no one but me. I can't make her feel better. I don't even know how to talk to her. I can't make it right for her. I can't even make it right for myself. I'm her only protection. I can't tell her that.

Sometimes she screams so loud I wonder if anyone else can hear her.

I still have the attacks after I go to sleep, but now it happens at different times in the night. Just knowing what causes them doesn't make them go away.

My husband gets up and sits with me when I think I'm going to die. I get sweaty and clammy. I can't talk. I just moan. He gets me ice cold wash cloths and rubs them on my neck and back. He puts ice in a cloth so I can rub it on the back of my neck.

• *April 23, 1992*

I know what it's like to believe you're going to be killed.

I know what it's like to run and try to get away after you've been dragged out of a car.

I know what it's like to beg and cry for your life.

I know what it's like to be knocked to the ground and to be torn inside as you're being attacked.

I know what it's like to be treated like the guilty one.

I know what it's like not to have anyone to talk about it to.

I know what it's like to be afraid to go for a walk, even if it's with someone.

I know what it's like to wake up because you're smothering and have to get outside because you know you can't breathe in the house.

I know what it's like to go to sleep at night, only to wake up a short time later throwing up and having diarrhea because of a recurring dream you've been having for the last 30 years.

I know what it's like to be told the rapist is out of prison and hunting for you and you believe there's no one to help you.

I know what it's like to live with guilt that's been placed on you for being a victim.

I know what it's like to be afraid to stand up as a mother on Mother's Day at church because you're afraid your sons are ashamed of you.

- *April 23, 1992*

I'm telling you all …
And I'm telling you from down here. There is no way out when you don't care. You can make your excuses, saying you don't have the time, but we know that it's all just a matter of the mind.

*It's been a long time since I wrote anything. I think I've stopped healing. Things are still going on ... I've been waiting for so long for someone to help me. (There is **no one**.) For three weeks now I've been way down in the valley ... not able to dig myself out. I've been lashing out at God and family. I'm so down ... I'm even failing God.*

I've always cared so much about helping people, and I've been there for a lot of them ... but where are these people when I need someone. I can't see them, I don't hear from them ... they're not there.

How can I ever get over my memories or my horrible fears of the rape?

My group sessions finally started, so I'm no longer seeing my therapist alone. We had two orientation classes, then took a two-week break before we actually started our group classes.

The two-week wait was difficult for me. I saw hurting women there. I felt classes had needed to start.

My group sessions were for abuse and rape victims. We were told, "The more the victim can talk about the abuse and rape, the more distance it puts between self and the pain and less identifies self as a victim and instead as a strong, capable adult. Shame exists in an environment of secrecy. When you begin to freely speak the truth about your life, your sense of shame will diminish."

I went to the group classes. I listened and listened to the pain from the women in my group. I saw the pain and shame in their faces. I saw how it was affecting their lives. They were all ages.

> **But she couldn't deal with their pain and ours, too. As they shared their experiences, she would be screaming. I wanted to run. I wanted to get as far away from their pain as I could. I didn't care where I ran, I just couldn't stand to hear them. I can't listen to any more! I see your pain and I can't help you! I can't even help myself.**
> **As they shared how they coped with their pain and shame, I could hear her screaming,**
> > **Run! Run! Run!**

I couldn't take any more. I left!

I told my therapist I was fine and didn't need to attend any more classes.

> **It was the only way I could shut her screaming up.**

I never shared the actual rape with either my therapist or my group.

She couldn't stop screaming long enough for me to tell it. She knew what happened on "that night," and she couldn't stand to hear it again.

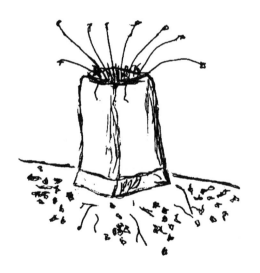

- *June 18, 1992*

I took shooting classes from a police officer, and my husband bought me a Smith & Wesson 38. I carried it with me at all times. Sometimes our life was unbearable because of the fear.

> Her crying and screaming continued. Sometimes I would try to help her; I would sing softly to her, but most of the time I still can't help myself.

Our fear lived on. I never looked at men when talking to them. I didn't know how to carry on a conversation with them.

> She was scared of them all. She would start screaming when one got near us. She believed everyone was a threat to us, and I tried not to reveal to her that I did, too.

- *June 19, 1992*

If you had ever met me, you would have found a smile on my fair freckled face most all of the time, but she saw behind the smile. Underneath the smile lay fear; behind the eyes that seemed to light up was fear. The heart lay behind a wall of cold fear.

When I am alone, all doors and bars are locked. Sometimes I would keep watching out the windows, while she cries softly. Being unable to comfort her, all I can do is reinforce the wall to keep me away from her.

• June 22, 1992

I received a summons for jury duty. As the selections were being made, a question was asked if anyone had been a victim of a vicious crime? I had to raise my hand. Before a large group of prospective jurors, I said, "I'm a rape survivor." You could have heard a pin drop. Inside I was dying of shame. Of course, I wasn't chosen.

> She alone knew the shame I felt, and she started screaming, "We're a victim, not a criminal."

For days I was depressed and ashamed, and for days she screamed and cried, wanting to be heard.

> She screamed, "We're innocent, we're not guilty." But there was no one to hear, no one to care because she could feel the wall around her being closed in tighter. I was burying her so deep no one would ever hear her.

What happens when I'm called up again for jury duty? It never ends.

• June 24, 1992

When I left Arkansas after the trial, I never wanted to go back. I didn't ever want to stand in front of all those people that I loved, because I didn't want them to be ashamed of me. I was afraid I wouldn't be able to keep my mask in place in front of them. Many of them were at the trial, but I was so emotional during the trial I wasn't sure how they felt about me. So, for years I've stayed away from them, never knowing how they felt.

When I finally went back, I had my mask firmly in place. No one was able to see me behind it. I don't know if they realized I was hiding from them with my mask. But if I didn't allow them to get too close to me, I don't believe they could tell.

The only problem with this was that I had to stay away from the funerals of those I loved. I knew with all the grief I wouldn't be able to keep my mask firmly in place. Do the rest of my relatives and friends think I don't care because I wasn't at the funerals? I don't know. During at least one of the funerals, I went to bed for at least three days, not eating and drinking very little water.

So I did my suffering away from them because I was ashamed of the rape.

The last time I was there I had everything in place. I wore the best I have, and I never broke down because my mask will slip off if I cry.

Some day I want to tell them I love them all dearly. I thank all of you who were able to go to the trial. But it's too soon for me to tell them now because I'm still living behind the mask..

47

You can purchase the nicest clothes money can buy. You can buy all the best accessories to wear with those nice clothes. You may be able to add a few nice pieces of jewelry, but you have to wear the same old mask.

- *July 1, 1992*

I never read rape stories in the paper. Total avoidance is the way I spend my life. I never watch them in the movies or on TV.

It's possible to live in a crowd and be submerged in loneliness and not feel a part of anyone's life; I have and oftimes I still do.

- *July 2, 1992*

    What have I done to her? Has all her screaming made her deaf? She stopped living at 17 and became an emotional cripple. Have I also become deaf? No! I still react when I hear others speak of pain.

- *July 3, 1992*

I wonder if I had been somewhere else that fateful night, where would I be today? Would my life have been spent in fear? Would I be self-confident knowing who I am and where I was going? If I had been sick that night and stayed safely in the house, how much easier my life would have been.

Look what it's done to her; there would be no child within screaming in fear. She would be all grown up and we would be one. Instead, today she and I cry together. Our life seems to be constantly in fear. We don't know who we are, and we've never known where we're going.

- *July 4, 1992*

Can't sleep. Sick. I'm lying on the bathroom floor calling for my husband to wake up. He gets up out of bed and rushes to the kitchen door, opening it and unlocking the bars so I can get outside.

I get up off the floor, run to get outside. I spend the rest of the night outside lying on a recliner telling myself I can breathe.

• July 8, 1992

Sick. I'm lying on the bathroom floor; my husband is up sitting with me. I need air, and even though the windows are wide open, I feel like there's no air. He rushes to the kitchen for ice to rub on the back of my neck. I can only moan, "Pray, pray." He puts the ice on my back, on my neck, my forehead. Finally the throwing up and diarrhea begin. Afterwards I'm shaking cold and clammy. Finally I'm able to go back to bed and forget everything in sleep.

- *July 9, 1992*

   It's hot in the house; all the windows are open. It's July; it's supposed to be hot, but I can't stand to shut the windows and turn on the central air conditioning. I tell myself if the windows are wide open, I'm not closed in. I can't stand to be closed in.

   It reminds me of the rapist holding me down. I couldn't move! I couldn't breathe! I couldn't make him get off! I was smothering to death!

   My husband and two sons spend nearly every summer without air conditioning, even though we have central air conditioning. I have to be able to see that air is coming into the house. If the windows are shut, my mind tells me, "There's no air, there's no air!"

I never knew just how much the rape had affected my life until I started my diary. I had never allowed myself to think about the rape. I thought I had completely closed off that area of my life, never to think about it again. I found out keeping a diary was forcing me to deal with it. It was making me think about it. I didn't want to think about it. I didn't want to deal with it. It eroded any self-confidence I tried to build up.

Every family gathering I felt inferior. The rape was always between me and them. I never felt I was treated the same as my siblings. I felt I was always the outsider. My accomplishments were never as important as theirs. I never knew what my parents wanted from me, or if they wanted anything from me.

I just want it over. I want it gone from my life. I don't want pity. I want to be like you. Don't treat me different or inferior. Let me be a survivor, not a victim. I don't even know what sympathy is; I've never had it. Guilt, now I know what that is.

If I'm told to move on, get over it, I'll tell you that you don't know what you're talking about. It makes me angry; it makes me mad!

Tell her when she's screaming with fear to get over it. Tell her it's okay to trust and believe in people. She's never been able to do that. Tell her she doesn't have to live behind walls. Tell her to grow up. Tell her these things, and you will completely destroy her. She believed once. She trusted once.

- *July 12, 1992*

It's still hot and sticky out, and I'm still sick most nights. It's nothing new, but it gets old. The only time I allow myself to think about the "rape" is when I write in my diary. The rest of the time every wall is up. If I ever hear a sound from her, I pound on the wall until I can't hear her any more.

I don't want to hear her. I don't want to be sick. It's hard to keep trying to act natural.

No one wants to hear about this. I tried talking to a friend about this, but she never calls me, so I call her. I know she doesn't want to hear; she just listens because I've called her. So I'll not burden her with this any more. The next time she sees or hears from me, my mask will be in place, and all my walls will be up. I won't mention it to her any more.

• *July 15, 1992*

Sometimes I dream about a small ship. It comes into the harbor and picks up those who can't find their way. You take no baggage with you, neither mental nor physical. It takes you to a place where you don't have to remember any more. You don't ever come back because you would have to remember again.

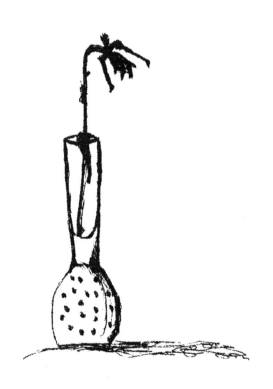

• *August 31, 1992*

Yes, I'm still operating on a survival level. I'm still afraid walking in the park with my husband and sons. I'm very careful not to let others close to her. So she's still isolated and I'm still trying to just stay alive.

I'm still having the attacks at night. I know "why," but I just haven't been able to stop them. They don't happen as much as they used to, but I still have them.

I haven't been able to forgive myself that I was raped. I can't forget that I wasn't able to protect her.

This savage crime happened in 1961.
Sharing my diary is very hard for me. I just want to be "set free."
I've taken my first step.

July 2000